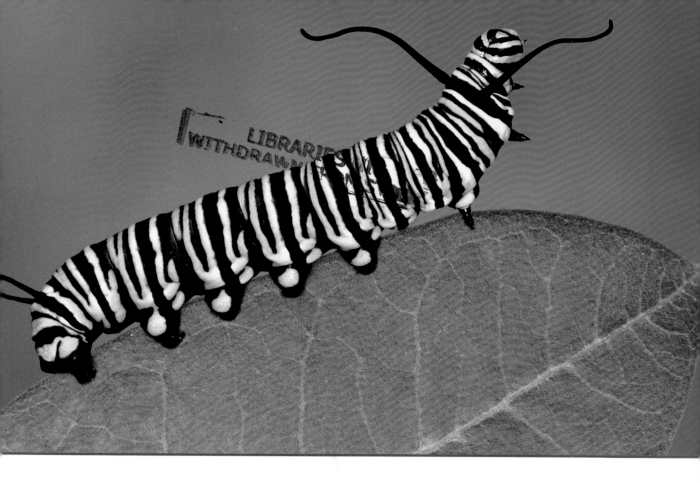

There are many different types of
baby minibeasts.

5

Eggs

egg

Some minibeasts lay eggs.

eggs

Butterflies lay eggs on leaves.

eggs

Mosquitoes lay eggs in water.

eggs

Bluebottles lay eggs on food.

silk case

egg

Some spiders put a silk case around their eggs.

silk

Some spiders hang their eggs from a silk thread.

Minibeast young

Many young minibeasts hatch
from eggs.

adult woodlouse

young woodlouse

Many young minibeasts look like adult minibeasts.

adult centipede

young centipede

Young centipedes look like
adult centipedes.

young spider

Young spiders look like adult spiders.

Changing minibeasts

young ladybird

adult ladybird

Some young minibeasts do not look like adult minibeasts.

larvae

Some eggs hatch into larvae.

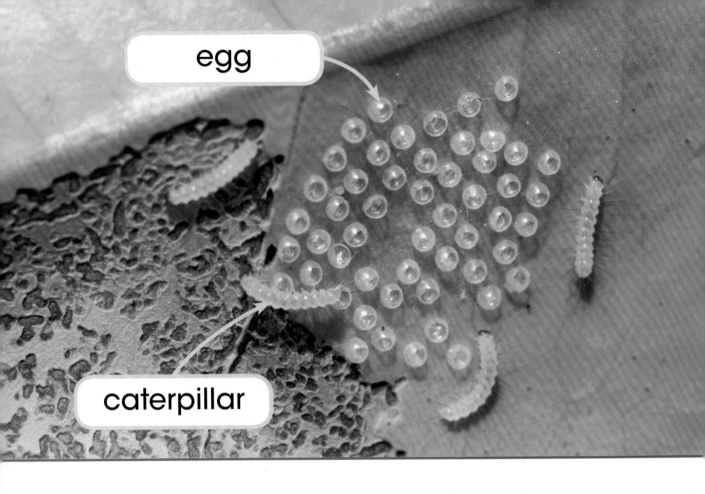

egg

caterpillar

A caterpillar is a type of larva.

A caterpillar grows and changes into a butterfly.

Caring for minibeast babies

bee larvae

Some insects take care of
their larvae.

young spider

Wolf spiders carry their young on their backs.

How big?

ladybird

mosquito

spider

Look at how big some of the minibeasts in this book can be.

Picture glossary

hatch break out of an egg

insect very small creature with six legs

larva minibeast baby that hatches from an egg. It does not look like an adult. More than one is larvae.

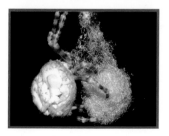
silk soft, strong material made by spiders and other minibeasts

Index

Notes to parents and teachers
Before reading
Make a list of minibeasts with the children. Try to include insects, arachnids (e.g. spiders), crustaceans (e.g. woodlice), myriapods (e.g. centipedes and millipedes), earthworms, slugs, and snails. Have they ever seen any minibeast eggs? Do they know what a butterfly egg hatches into?

After reading
- Get a butterfly kit for your classroom to watch how caterpillars grow and change into butterflies. Help the children to measure the caterpillars, and examine them under a magnifying glass. Ask the children to make a diary recording how the caterpillars change.
- Between spring and late summer you could go outside and hunt for minibeast eggs. Show the children how to look in soil, under stones, in dead leaves, and on leaves. If they find any eggs ask them to observe and record how many eggs there are, what shape and colour they are, and where exactly they were found.
- If the children find any eggs you could bring them into the classroom and put them into a pot along with some of the soil or leaves on which they were found. Ask the children to watch the eggs every day and see if any minibeasts hatch.